Mad Sestina King

David Spicer

FUTURECYCLE PRESS
www.futurecycle.org

Cover artwork by Nancy Clift Spicer with production assistance by Jo Clift; author photo by Nancy Clift Spicer; cover and interior book design by Diane Kistner; ITC Legacy Sans text with Tork titling

Library of Congress Control Number: 2020948023

Published by FutureCycle Press
Athens, Georgia, USA

ISBN 978-1-952593-07-9

For the Mad Sestina Queen

Contents

❧

❧❧

❧❧❧

❧❧❧❧

❦

Word Cruncher

I'm thinking outside the bowl.
No more strawberries, cereal and cream
for this word cruncher. They're not so super
anymore, plus the other day I told
myself a word braved is a word burned,
and a curd in the hand is worth two in the mush.

Suddenly you're telling me to hush
hush, tweet starlet, that I can't bowl
tonight? Is it something earned,
like dancing at the last concert by Cream
(or any other power-group, truth be cold),
as long as I can stop by the super-

market before I scream *Super! Super!*
while I listen to *Breaking in the Wind?*
I think I'll drop acid just to take a hold
of myself and get a bowl
haircut without shaving cream:
it'll look good if the barber turns

my head just right, so it resembles an urn—
better yet, a Warhol can of soup, or
a plate of tacos, nachos and sour cream
with *The Old Man Takes a Pee*
nearby, that, for the tenth time today, bowls
me over more than *To Whom the Mole Told.*

But, one to eat crow and tell,
I admit I have a lesson to learn:
whenever I choose to write, my vowels
slay the lice, pretend they're superior
to consonants that leak secrets from tushes,
though they can't digest ice cream.

And I, their hungry owner, can only scream
when I blow my nose and not tell
you that a tart is a baloney hunter.
I might as well drink a smoothie of ferns
for breakfast, lunch, snacks and supper,
slurping it slowly, and from a bowl.

I love cream if it's dour, if it's burned.
That tells me it's no longer bold or super,
but I covet crushed words crunched outside a bowl.

Nights Hobble Along
Like Crippled Cows Past My Bed

The first few minutes I wake
after three hours of sleep
tease me. I feel myself drift
into a gradual surrender
and Morpheus deigns to be kind.
For an hour. Then my eyes open.

I don't want my eyes open,
not at two when no one's awake.
Except for insomniacs of my kind:
shift workers resisting sleep—
sometimes, though, surrendering—
or truckers who can't afford to drift

and swerve on roads into snow drifts
at three a.m. under a frigid sky open
to different forms of eyelid surrender.
These thoughts keep me awake.
Why can't I begin to sleep?
Why can't I ride this cow, the crippled kind

hobbling through the nights of no kind-
ness, enough to feel the freedom of a drifter
who'd settle for a drugged sleep
or wander into a Dunkin' Donuts open
at four in the morning when the city's awake
for speed freaks who can't surrender?

Five a.m. Work creeps up—no surrender.
I debate searching for night hawks kind
enough to talk, but are any awake?
Do I surf the web, seek tips on drifting
into a dream paradise, open
to almost everyone who sleeps?

Sunrise blinds me: I can't sleep,
since dawn is a stranger to surrender,
now that the city morning opens
to sleepers no longer sleepers but kind
workers, students, police and drifters
who swap happy hellos, barely awake.

Sleep, are you now kind,
as surrender slowly drifts
to my half-open eyes, as if I'm at a wake?

The Patagonia in My Mind

I haven't traveled any roads
outside America, nor found riches
from other lands. In my mind, on a seagull,
I do that, fitting my legs into stirrups
as she flies over the selvages
of Chile and Argentina: Patagonia.

What a marvelous word. *Pat-a-go-nia.*
I see in my mind the roads
of mountains along selvages,
and imagine riches
I manage to stir up
from the vantage point of my seagull.

But I'm no Jonathan Livingston Seagull.
I can't fly with wings to Patagonia,
nor be a gaucho with boots in the stirrups
of a horse galloping the roads,
who whistles and lassos the riches
I'd love to discover along the selvages.

The treasures I'd salvage
if I could, as though a seagull.
No, I have only a fantasy of riches
unique to hills and valleys of Patagonia,
land of a thousand rocky roads
known only to a romantic in his stirrups:

I mount my stallion, slip into the stirrups,
trotting around the selvages
down lonely expanses of cold roads.
I gaze at the clouds shaped like seagulls
floating over this Eldorado, Patagonia,
which hides more than silver or gold riches:

in a small ranch my true riches—
a wife, two boys readying legs into the stirrups
of the three horses hidden in Patagonia,
a trio I salvaged
like a beautiful nomad seagull
who remembered every remote road

from her searches for rich selvages,
who didn't need stirrups: a seagull
roaming the Patagonia in my mind of roads.

My Commencement Address

I've not entered the wilderness,
nor visited any monkeys,
but I love innocent faces
of those who possess a smaller brain
than we do, who didn't discover fire
as we did or learn its significance.

Mankind realized its significance:
we left the wilderness,
said goodbye to gifts—but not fire—
and goodbye to the monkeys,
who possessed their brains
to breed, to live and to face

the world, recognize their own faces.
The same as each of us: who is significant,
with a less or more intelligent brain,
and who conquers the wilderness.
Or if we consider ignorant monkeys.
That way, we won't feel the heat of fire,

we remain cold, not "fired-
up" like those who display anger in faces
and leap to the nearest tree like monkeys.
Who don't understand they can signify
they want to remain in the wilderness.
That they can transcend the fact their brains

live in their bodies, that brains
are important. And if an employer ever fires
you, don't fume, or enter the wilderness
or allow what you feel to inhabit your face.
Benignly proclaim, *I accept this,* and signify
it by choosing not to monkey

around every day. Remember: monkeys
evolved into our kind with a small brain.
Know what those ramifications signify.
It's not your only gift: you own a fire
inside yourselves, so face
that fact, don't fear the wilderness

like monkeys once did. Keep that fire
within your brain, love the faces
significant in your life, your wilderness.

Thoughts on Meditation

I've never practiced meditation,
my body neither supple nor limber.
Anything as disciplined and formal
as closing eyes steals minutes
from a life that contracts,
that locks me behind a door in this city.

I don't jog, like many city
dwellers. I learn about life from *Meditations*,
or try to, for I think my mind contracts
when a hint surfaces. I limber
up my thoughts and think of minute
details to engage the formal

logic of abstract thought. It's like a formal:
I don't attend fancy functions in the city,
not used to intricacies so minute
I can't entertain meditations
about parties. I'd rather think of the lumber
my redneck son utilizes when not contracting

diseases or watching his wife's contractions
for the eighth time as if a foregone formality.
He yells, *Come on, baby, you're limber
enough! Pop 'im out so we can blow this city!*
I wish he'd practice meditation
or escape to a bar for a few minutes,

like a clerk on a break from twenty minutes
of a battle involving a contract
between a landlord and a bookseller meditating
too much, ignoring language formal
but deadly to a blasé boor living in the city.
Who thinks he can sell his books in a limbo,

and not pay a landlord who needs lumber
to fix his tenant's cafe, *Coffee in Minutes.*
He brews fast money in the growing city:
expanding exponentially, with few contracts,
the cafe possesses an ambience that's informal,
where patrons can read *Meditations.*

Whether my world's contracting or limber,
I pause a few minutes without formalities,
stay in my apartment and read *Meditations.*

Enamel Cross

When the art-dealer deacon asked the enamelist
if he'd like a commission to craft a cross
for a gold cross's center, the artist thought
and said, *Yes,* in the belief
his talents could enhance an object of the spirit
and contribute to the church

that he perceived as more than a church.
A venue of stained glass and enamel,
one that allowed him to celebrate the spirit,
for he, like other members, had crosses
to bear, giving him faith to believe
in a power that supported his thoughts.

He began, immersed himself in thought
about art, color, life, church.
In the past he had drifted with no belief
system, one that could guide and enamel
his collection of days onto the cross
of his larger life: his inner spirit.

As days progressed, his spirits
wavered, transforming thoughts
of a cross to an image of a cross
within a larger cross, one the church
could cherish, one he'd relish as an enameler.
He tackled the task with vigor, not believing

matter could conquer his mind. He believed
his art lifted him into a spiritual
realm, where a higher source enameled
his skills to create something he thought
presentable to the church.
When he finished, he polished the cross.

On the altar, the crimson cross
glistened in the gold cross. He believed
it a work of sublime art for his church,
a sanctuary for humans and spirits,
where prayer complemented thinking
important to the enamelist.

Later, the artist designed a cross as spiritual
as the finished cross marrying belief with thought:
another church's medallion, in a deep blue enamel.

for Joe Clift

A Football

Before I passed the sixth grade,
I received one of my rare honors:
the school awarded me a football
for Safety Patrolman of the Week.
Indifferent to useless gifts,
I placed it on a shelf in my room.

My brother and I shared that bedroom.
Bruce, a jock, a ninth grader,
held the leather gift
as though honored
to feel strong, not weak,
stroking the elliptical ball.

I didn't value the football,
ignored it in the room.
My brother, staring at it for weeks,
decided to gradually
identify the ball with his honor,
thinking he deserved the gift.

One day Bruce punctured it. His gift
to me. Stuck an ice pick, wore a ballsy
sneer devoid of honor.
Standing in *his* room,
he glowered with great
contempt for my perceived weakness.

You're a pussy, a weakling.
You don't deserve this gift.
No, I didn't get high grades
as a player carrying a football,
evading tackles with room
to spare, honorably.

I cared about honor
but didn't ache every week,
or watch men fight for room
to move to give themselves the gift
of a fought-over football,
in order to possess a brutal grace.

Decades later Bruce honored me with a gift:
Hey, weakling, here's a football.
I stuck it in a storage room, degrading it.

Warriors

My needy sister Tina and mother
Lori waged ferocious battle—
I don't know why—until Lori died
of several strokes and loneliness.
Tina reacted by shoplifting
and ignoring her cats and dogs.

I imagine you're calling me a dog
for revealing laundry of my mother
and Tina's career as a shoplifter,
but I grew cynical from their battles,
and we all fight demons of loneliness,
wait for the day we don't want to die.

Tina and Lori fought until their deaths.
One day Tina sicced Mike, her bulldog,
onto ornery Lori, but Mike ran away lonely,
and the next day my mother
retaliated with a new tactic, battling
Tina with words: *You scummy shoplifter,*

but Tina retorted, *I know you shoplift,*
too, Polyanna bitch! Why don't you die?!
All their lives, Tina and Lori battled
themselves, too, and, with dogged
focus, felt that other rotten mother-
fuckers deserved misery and loneliness

more than they did, these loners
who craved conflict and shoplifting.
Tina the daughter, Lori the mother
loved to act crazy, like dyeing
their hair so purple the bulldog
Mike returned for more battles.

When Tina and Lori renewed their battles
against the other and loneliness,
they blamed the world for the prodigal dog,
but celebrated with a binge of shoplifting
books about dying, death and dyes,
which pleased my sister and mother.

That final battle and spree of shoplifting
fueled Tina's loneliness over Lori's death
after she yelled, *You're a dog of a mother!*

Michelangelo's Handshakes

We're all fond of different gestures:
men, upon meeting, trade handshakes.
Teenagers might make a point
when angry by flashing middle fingers,
while some women exchange letters
to discuss the great Michelangelo.

One person—Michelangelo,
my misanthropic uncle—refused gestures
of goodwill, thought writing letters
worthless and when exchanging handshakes
he'd squeeze other men's fingers
so hard they'd say, *You trying to prove a point,*

asshole, and just what is your point?
Everybody knew him as Michelangelo,
but now they didn't have strong fingers,
now that he made this gesture.
I told my uncle his handshakes
had the effect of letter

bombs, and he should write letters
of apology to explain the point
that nothing made less sense than handshakes
between men, who despised Michelangelo.
You're so full of it, boy. I love my gesture
of squeezing the hell out of fingers,

and here's a middle finger
to writing wimpy letters....
I saw in my uncle's eyes a small gesture
that more than proved his point
many men see themselves as Michelangelo,
a man with a marble-cold handshake.

What was in his eyes? Not handshakes.
Something I can't begin to finger,
any more than my uncle Michelangelo
figured why I thought letters
could verify the vapid point
that one gesture is superior to another gesture.

A handshake means no more, no less than a letter.
Fingers aren't meant to squeeze, but to point.
And Uncle Michelangelo's name was a gesture.

Grandpa Jonas

I believed my ancestors were American Indians
rather than Irish or Scotch,
but neither assumption proved correct:
some migrated from Iberia, speaking
to nobody on the ship until settling in Buffalo,
New York, working and fucking

because they liked to work and fuck—
wherever they emigrated from, even if India.
Later, my grandparents moved to Buffalo,
Wyoming, where Jonas concocted Scotch
eggs. He adored those babies, couldn't speak
without eating one first—he thought it the correct

custom out West, and nobody dared correct
him, lest he exclaim, *Fuck*
this, I'll just close down my speak-
easy and invite all my Indian
friends to liberate the bourbon and scotch.
He owned the hottest temper in both Buffalos:

in a Wyoming pasture, drunk, he rode a buffalo,
and a friend advised, *You're not riding correctly,*
Jonas. Man, I think you'd scotch
praying or royally fuck
up how to talk to local Indians.
Jonas said, *Don't tell me how to speak,*

or I'll choke you with these spokes.
Afterwards, people in Buffalo
steered clear of my grandpa, who loved Indian
bikes, and neighbors didn't correct
him—he'd infer they frowned on fucking
savages. He thought Scots

in the area wouldn't dare eat a Scotch
bonnet or a Scotch egg, and speaking
of eating, Grandpa Jonas ate while fucking.
He told me on his deathbed, winked like a buffalo.
At the end, Jonas mumbled in correct
slang: he called Native Americans Indians,

and in his casket a bottle of scotch sporting a buffalo
label with a note spoke for him: *Don't correct
me and don't fucking preach to me about Indians!*

The Pizza Hut Twins

wear wrinkled uniforms
to Pizza Hut almost every day,
taking turns as alpha, marching
on a sidewalk, one heavier than the other,
both owning the same face from parents
who looked so similar friends called them twins.

Their daughters are identical twins
who don't like uniforms.
Do they blame their parents
for advising them each day is a new day,
that they mustn't leave the other,
one walking behind in a march

toward Pizza Hut all months except March?
Could they separate as twins,
travel to distant cities, so far from the other
they'd forget about their jobs and uniforms?
When I see them—almost every day—
I wonder if they take turns as parent,

whether they speak to their parents
over the phone during months besides March.
Or, if they return home, how many days
they visit as twins,
whether they parade their uniforms
to prove they're not separate from the other.

I wish I'd ask if they feel different from others,
if they want to disown their parents
and marry twins who wouldn't uniformly
walk to work every month, even March.
I ask myself if twins marry twins
when I see the Pizza Hut twins on weekdays.

I'm saving more questions for some day
that I don't feel like I'm one of these *others*:
yes, I'm a twin who can't separate from his twin.
I'm the dominant, so I'll play parent,
cajole my brother to march
to the twins and ask about uniforms.

Day in, day out, he and I curse our parents,
how we're unlike the others: not marching
like the Pizza Hut twins in their uniforms.

Spaghetti for Holidays

Every Christmas day my wife's brother
and his wife invite us to eat ham
along with all kinds of pies, rolls,
and other food designed for weight
gain. Then they go visit the mean lady
at the gym, who tortures and molds

them into fit specimens, not fitting fat molds.
This year we've invited them and a brother
and sister—an English gentleman and lady—
to our home for a meal other than ham:
ground beef, sauce, peppers—worth waiting
for, served with wine and humor that rolls

off tongues with the taste of spaghetti, and rolls
that can't sit unbaked for an hour lest they mold
and threaten to make one prone to gain weight.
Belinda and Max, sister and brother,
commented the meal wasn't the same ham,
the kind eaten with a neighbor who wasn't a lady,

who gossiped, lonely because she knew no ladies
who would share tales about ex-husbands or rolls,
not to mention a slice of annual ham
served in a damp house with black and green mold
that spread since a diabetic brother
had died in bed from too much weight.

No, Max and Belinda, thin, unworried about weight,
liked spaghetti away from the non-lady,
and my wife didn't say, *Eat, eat, eat,* to her brother,
who drank glasses of wine, ate spaghetti, a few rolls
that made him unfit, breaking the mold
of someone who drinks no wine and eats little ham.

He'd vow, on New Year's Day, to stop eating ham
or food that posed a problem for weight,
food so delicious or tempting it molded
him into someone who couldn't escape mean ladies
making him regret his intake of wine and rolls
and wish he'd eaten no spaghetti like a lean brother

should. They didn't eat ham to spite the mean lady,
but gained weight from spaghetti and rolls,
blasé about molding wives, husbands and brothers.

A Game of Chess

Ironic that the powerful piece is the Queen
and the weakest is the King
in a game of sixty-four spaces
and an infinite number of moves.
It's a lot like life, my father explained,
but in chess, players have more than one chance

to play the game that relies on skill, not chance.
Ironic, too, that I've viewed women as queens:
I didn't need a misogynist to explain
women to me. He felt they treated him like a pawn
to achieve their goals, that they thought eight moves
ahead of him and didn't give him any space

in his life, treating him as if he came from outer space.
Sometimes women won't grant me one chance
to say something to them so moving
they can't help but see in my gaze they're queens,
and I'd do anything to love them in a rook-
guarded castle that needs no explaining.

But that's sexist and stupid, feminists explain,
and I'd answer, *That's just me, I'm spaced-
out.* I'm a dreamer, like a knight
in dull armor willing to sacrifice to chance
if he could court his queen
who'd adore him, allow him to move

around without thinking eight moves
ahead. I've never believed chess explains
life or life imitates chess, even if a queen
poses as a woman and doesn't care about space,
whose secret desire is to name her child *Chance*
after she's blessed and married by a bishop.

I'm not sure I want a king's treatment.
A king isn't allowed many moves
in either game. He's given few chances
to escape situations, to offer explanations
that provide him with open spaces
to embrace his woman, his queen.

I don't envy kings in chess. No explaining
needed. In life, I move for enough space
to have a chance when I meet her: a queen.

The Mermaid and the Airplane

If I could give you an ocean
with lighthouses and buoys,
nights full of storms and stars,
days windy with birds in flight,
I'd snap my fingers and you
wouldn't portray a mermaid.

You dislike playing mermaids.
Living near the moody ocean
frightens the gentle part of you,
makes you grab buoys
or envy gulls taking flight
to kiss a sky full of stars.

I wish I could give you a star
for the time you acted as mermaid
on a choppy airplane night flight
over ten countries and two oceans
that became calm and buoyed
when the wings felt light from you.

About that night: I never asked you
if you conferred with clouds and stars,
wanted them to be your strong buoys.
I watched you in the role of mermaid
even though you weren't in an ocean,
but on a steel bird's turbulent flight.

I won't wonder if thought of flight
ever crossed your mind, made you
wish to be near the moody ocean
instead of discussing with stars
virtues of an airplane-mermaid
playing the part of a scaled buoy.

In an airplane not used to buoys
until that dark, cloud-kissing flight
when passengers met a mermaid
who wasn't a mermaid, but you,
dreaming one day of your stardom,
an actress who slept by an ocean.

The buoy that scary night—you—
now beyond flight, now a star,
once a mermaid afraid of oceans.

Honeymoon

We thrived on romantic
evenings, complete with wine—
sweet and punchy Pinot Noir—
lived in France and Italy,
kissing the other's forehead,
didn't assign blame

to the other for anything, blame
with many labels except romantic.
When I kissed your tanned forehead
I thought of that wine-
colored birthmark shaped like Italy
on the actor in a famous film noir

I can't remember. Too many noirs
linger in my memory. I can't blame
you for that. I watched them in Italy
with no inclination toward romance
and lush red wines
that I drank nights for a heady

effect that pressed my forehead.
I hope I didn't rouse my bête noire
disguised as a favorite wine-
lover. He reveled in blaming
me for clumsy words after I romanced
you over a secluded table in Italy.

We called our memories Italian,
didn't care why, headed
toward another night of romance,
watched a classic noir,
not grasping the definition of *blame*.
We sipped hundred-dollar glasses of wine

before loving with moans, wines
that embellished France and Italy,
before we nicknamed the other *The Blamer,*
threw anything at the other's foreheads:
a dozen scratchy discs of film-noirs
or a crateful of detective or romance

novels. Weary of wine, kisses to foreheads,
we forgot Italy, film and Pinot Noirs,
blamed each other for our loss of romance.

Before You Say Farewell

It's my sincere hope
that you'll acquiesce
and decide to break bread
with me before you say *Farewell*.
If you do, I'll chop wood
and, then, we can reminisce, quietly.

We did nothing quietly—
without reason, without hope
that we could be more than wooden
puppets of each other's Ackeresque
tendencies. So, before saying *Farewell*,
allow me to offer a drink or bread

if you decide that bread's
the best food to eat when quietly
preparing a fond *Farewell*.
Do you want to leave, Hope?
Could I make a gesture of acquiescence
that might make you feel wooed

again? Tell me what that would
be, either in narrow or broad
terms. I'll listen. To acquiesce
to your wishes. I'll sit quietly
as you speak, hope
to remain silent and fare well

with you. Can I prevent your *Farewell*?
Chop five cords of wood
for winter and hope against hope
that you won't leave? Don't brood.
I know you slowly and quietly
consider my offers to acquiesce

because after I do acquiesce
to prevent a *Farewell,*
I take advantage of your quietude
and treat you like chopped wood
or a stale loaf of bread.
So, I ask now, Hope,

can I acquiesce like waiting wood,
or will you say, *Farewell, bread*
won't quietly feed my mind, as you hope?

If You Might Be Dying

In a world dying,
it's unwise to possess sentiment,
pursue an impulsive romance,
or love birds, cats and dogs.
Your fragile part, the heart,
may burst from your chest and risk

flopping on the asphalt at great risk
to you. You'll be dying
and literally heart-
less, thus incapable of sentiment.
That heart is now dessert for dogs
that possess no romance

in their bones, no wish to romance
a cat or a bird or a hydrant without risk-
ing their nature as loyal dogs.
And, friend, if you might be dying,
die without regret, or sentiment,
hold your friend—your heart—

for dear life. Rush to the room where hearts
recover, where you may relearn romance
despite the exhausted world, sentimental-
izing what remains left of time. Risk
a memory of your lover dyeing
his hair red, holding you, your two dogs,

hugging them with a wan smile. A dogged
desire to deem the heart
larger than living or dying,
as your lover lives for romance
when he gazes into your eyes, risks
believing that life lacks sentiment.

And as you recall that love, that sentiment,
forget if each of you acted like dogs,
hitting, biting, exposed the other to risk.
Forget the times each of you lacked a heart
to share and that no dreamy, romantic
counselor prevented unavoidable dying

with sentiment. No, hide your tired heart
where dogs can't sniff out the romance
of risk that's unafraid of living or dying.

The Boat

We're all in the same boat,
Ada, a pessimist, told me. Young,
I didn't believe her, thought I was blessed.
Thirty years later, in a survivors'
room, I listen to the television silence time.
I agree with Ada, dead of breast cancer.

Here doctors warn us about brain cancer,
but my headphones lull me like a boat
on a calm river. My sick wife, killing time,
solves crosswords, not feeling old or young,
and I watch the different survivors,
wanting to believe we're blessed.

Are we? Are you blessed?
Have you, a friend or a lover waited in a cancer
clinic watching a repeat of *Survivor,*
judged cast members who connive in a canoe,
some of them old, or hot, or cold or young,
and crossing fingers it's not their time?

I hope nobody here worries about time:
not the teacher who might feel blessed,
the mother who loves her five youngsters,
the pin-striped banker with melanoma
who dreams of his ten-million-dollar yacht,
or the bald twenty-year-old smiling to survive.

Thinking about these survivors,
I listen to Cohen's *Closing Time.*
We're all in the same boat.
That was Ada's version of *Nobody's blessed.*
Life'll destroy us, whether it's leukemia
late in life or a car crash when we're young.

All of us wish we were younger
than we are, but we survive.
So far, we might dodge cancer,
hope to spend more time
breathing air that's blessed,
drifting in our boat.

Nobody's young, running out of time
to survive. Some of us have been blessed
to escape cancer in this sinking boat.

Breve Latte and Plantation Shutters

Twice a day for a year Nancy loved to drive
to Starbucks and buy five-dollar coffees,
bring them home to smell and drink.
She nursed containers of breve latte,
talked of buying plantation shutters
for our house windows, how her dream

was to live and dream
with no cares. This goal gave her drive,
so much drive it made her friends shudder,
so much she'd need cups of coffee
for her nerves and focus—mostly the latter.
She tried gin, vodka and other clear drinks

but couldn't find the perfect drink.
She said liquor made her lose her dreamer's
gaze, so she'd sip breve latte
all day. That was fine—she said she'd drive
to Starbucks twice for custom-made coffee
instead of buying expensive shutters.

Months later she decided how to buy shutters:
she told me she could drink
the wonderful coffee
and fulfill her passionate dream
by saving all that money and not drive
to Starbucks for her breve latte.

She said, *I'll make my own breve latte,*
saving money and buying shutters
in months with single-minded, intense drive.
She said she'd bask in the pleasure of drinking
her own—cheaper, better—in the house, dream
of one-of-a-kind, shutter-sipping coffee.

Bravo! I cheered. Nancy ordered coffee
pots, creamers and ten-buck aerolattes
as steps toward her dream
of buying cream-hued plantation shutters.
Within seven to twelve months of drinking
cups of her home blend—and not driving

for coffee—she ordered plantation shutters
while making breve latte to drink
with new goals brewing, dreams requiring drive.

Cruciverbalist

Every night Nancy
lounges in her blue chair across
from me, fitting words
into small squares,
and asks for right
answers to opaque clues.

Often I don't offer a clue,
even when the answer is *Nancy*
or so obvious it's staring right
at me and I'm cross-
eyed, feeling like a square
unaware of the power in words.

*What's the Greek word
for* oak? I don't have a clue
about the letters in the squares,
reply, *Give me an easy one, Nancy,
like a short word for* cross.
She smiles: I'm rarely right

with my guesses, as though it's a rite
of passage every night to guess words,
as though they're hanging on a cross
ready to catch the correct clue:
Sluggo's girlfriend—Nancy.
But sometimes we're at square

one, when little is square,
and we begin again, try to write
the correct letters Nancy
knows, even the final word
unrelated to the clue
for ninety-nine across.

Both she and I are never cross:
we fill every last square
from vague clues,
elicit some right
solutions, providing words
that satisfy Nancy.

So, whether five across, left or right,
penciled-in squares compose words,
despite clues that are nonsense to Nancy.

The Master and Her Artists

Sandra is proud of the artists,
inviting them to her studio of color.
Nine women draw and paint
figures, portraits and landscapes,
each a student of shadow and light,
one my quiet wife.

Today, I drove my wife—
who all her life has studied artistic
maneuvers of brush against light—
to the teacher's den of color,
where white walls are landscaped
with charcoals, contours and paintings.

Sandra cherishes her role of teacher-painter—
I've learned that much from my wife—
like a gardener adores the green landscape.
She offers critiques of her protégés' art
with a droll wit and charm that colors
wise advice not taken lightly

by these purveyors of darkness and light.
The nameless women have painted
before, explored mysteries of color,
and rely on Sandra (including my wife)
to provide them with artful
techniques to portray landscapes.

Outside, a man waves—the landscaper—
and Sandra smiles, flicks a lighter
to a cigar, says, *Oh, that's Art*
acting like a man: he wants to paint
the house. The women, even my wife,
inquire in unison, *What color?*

I love Art, but he doesn't know color
any more than I know landscaping.
One of the women (not my wife),
grins, her eyes turquoise in the light,
and jokes, *We could color and paint*
the house until it's a work of art.

About Art, Sandra says. She adds a color
to the painting of her landscape,
providing more light. *I'm his wife.*

for Nancy Cheairs

Ginger Woman

I like a helluva lot of ginger
in what I eat, whether a heel
of a lover, or a fat baker's
muffins. And if he farts wind,
well, he might be a spy
or loves Screamin' Jay Hawkins.

Maybe he's fond of Ronnie Hawkins
and his Hawks, I don't know: Ginger
helps me a lot to spy
on all men. It more than heals
me, it's a trouper when I wind
down from some Ginger Baker.

I just strut next door, ask the baker
what kind of spicy pie he's hawkin'.
Well, look what the damn wind
blew in, it's the Queen of Ginger,
Ginger herself, he says. *Here's a heel,*
honey, it'll more than perk up your spy-

chops. Sure, he knows I spy
on him and all the Parisian bakers,
but he doesn't say, *Bitch, heel!*
Instead, he recites Stephen Hawking
and coos *sooo* softly, *Awww, Ginger,*
you and I—we could ride the wind

on a flying camel until the damn wind
died. Well, I hint, *you* could *spy*
on punters who love ginger
like I do, plus the bakers
who pretend they're hawkin'
up some old green heel

56

of a bread loaf. But he's not a heel,
my dough boy who loves straddlin' the wind—
unlike all those bastards named Hawkins.
I have the edge, though: they don't know I spy
on them and the Parisian bakers.
I pretend I'm taste-testing ginger.

I'm a heel, hell yes, and hell yes, I'm a spy.
I'll wind you up and wind you down if you're a baker.
Last name first, first name last? Hawkins, Ginger.

J. P. Donleavy 1926-2017

Femme Fatale

I gave you close comfort.
Please don't grovel.
You loved yourself
too much to see my beauty:
it destroys dreaming fools
who don't think with their heads,

And I *didn't* give you head.
If it's any comfort,
I've met sillier fools.
They snivel, cry, grovel
at the sight of my beauty.
Morons like yourself.

Claim you weren't yourself,
sweep me out of your head,
find a brilliant beauty
who'll give you physical comfort,
but don't let her see you grovel,
for fear she, too, thinks you foolish.

Stop making foolhardy
choices, find your witty self.
Or *do* let me live in your head,
and make a habit of groveling.
You won't receive any comfort,
least of all from a beautiful

femme fatale. This is what's beautiful:
you're a crotch-cogitating fool.
Deny that, if you feel comfortable.
Or better yet, be your selfish
self like I am, escape your head,
and trick women to grovel.

Make them think you're lovers, groveller:
they'll line up for your beauty.
Shake your curly blond head
and they'll pursue you more—the fools—
convinced you're self-
fulfilled enough to give more than comfort.

Again, don't grovel, you naïve fool,
know that beauty isn't self-
less. Clear your head, spread comfort.

He Called Himself *Smart*

I knew a bright fellow,
Smart, obsessed with how smart
he was. *I have a stellar IQ,*
he bragged to me without excuse.
Something's in my genes,
he said, *that conquers mountains*

and countries without mountains.
Today, I identify the fellow,
his body on the slab in blue jeans.
He thought he was the smartest
man in every room. *Never say* Excuse
me, he advised, *because your IQ*

doesn't need manners. On cue,
I visualized the Smoky Mountains,
or began to sneeze as an excuse
to escape lessons of this smug fellow
who couldn't believe how much smarter
he was than his girlfriend, Jean,

who—for him—pulled down her jeans.
Jean, sensing he had a low EQ,
seduced him into thinking she wasn't smart,
lured him to a remote mountain
cabin, the sky gray and soil fallow,
saying as she locked its door, *Excuse*

me, Smart. I have no excuse
except I have to buy a pair of jeans
for a date with a brilliant fellow,
one in my deep, dangerous queue.
Have fun in these foggy mountains!
And if you survive me, tell me if it smarts

to freeze where Don Juans smarter
than you have died, where there's no excuse
for thinking you're the best mountain
expert. Strange how the corpse wore jeans
of the heartbreaker with higher quotients
than his: she could seduce any fellow.

Poor Smart. In tight-fitting jeans,
he had one excuse: a low EQ
that left him a dead mountain fellow.

In My Younger Years I Loved the Oboe

Not many people play the oboe.
Years ago, wanting to draw
it, I hiked two miles to Tower
Records and found the issue moot:
not many musicians cross the Rubicon
toward that woodwind and caress it, nor hoard

tapes of concerts that even a hoarder
won't keep. I didn't find any oboe
pictures, but later saw one of the Rubicon,
an accurate and admirable drawing
I liked so much I turned mute
for a moment. In the foreground, a tower

loomed above the river, towered
over the landscape and the hordes
as an army pushed them into a moat
and a lone figure held an oboe-
like instrument near the draw-
bridge. In it, Caesar crossed the Rubicon

and I, too, decided to cross the Rubicon
and bought the picture of the tower.
I arrived home, placed it in a drawer,
forgot it, lost for decades in my hoard
of objects connected to the oboe,
rendering my attraction to it moot.

But one night, in a dark mood,
I remembered the picture of the Rubicon
and the man with the oboe,
searched for it, knocked down a tower
of paper and found it buried in the hoard
at the bottom of the drawer:

I studied it, began to draw,
my imitation of the illustration moot:
I should have kept it buried in my hoard,
or tossed it into the depths of the Rubicon.
Depressed, I listened to Cohen's *Tower*
of Song, feeling like a discarded oboe

nobody wants to draw, or the lonely Rubicon,
mute and cold, flowing beside an empty tower
before a horde, nobody in it with an oboe.

Elegy for a Rock 'n' Roll Life

Lou Reed, you walked on the wild
side, one of my music heroes
in the same way arch poet Delmore
Schwartz was to you: deciding to live
the life desired, whether with velvet
friends, or with dope in needled alleys.

You first wrote songs in Tin Pan Alley,
but ascended quickly, grew wildly
when Warhol sponsored you and the Velvets:
god-angels to punks, you loved heroin,
roamed the underground of your lives,
something you learned from Delmore.

A poet I knew studied with you and Delmore:
a kind teacher with a pained wince, his alleys
were the hallways of academic life.
We talked about the meek, not the wild,
side of poets who weren't their own heroes,
those who thought their tongues were velvet.

Lou, you had quite a ride with the Velvets,
leaving after many battles—much like Delmore
may have had if he'd been a rock 'n' roll hero:
waiting for the man in dangerous alleys,
a transformer on dirty boulevards, wild
from all of tomorrow's parties in a dark life.

You may have lived in a different life
as a poet who danced on carpets of velvet,
but I doubt it: a rock 'n' roll poet is wild
enough to be immortal, like Delmore,
who, like you, didn't need friends or allies,
because you two were your own heroes.

Later, you loved Laurie, a poet, your heroine
singing she'd be your mirror, let you live a life
of music, play it with her above a dank alley,
wearing nothing but luscious robes of velvet,
to honor the closet rock 'n' roller Delmore,
who taught you a life lived is a life lived wild.

Lou, my rock 'n' roll hero, my premier Velvet:
you could really live, like the great Delmore,
not in college alleys, but on the side that's wild.

Redhead Limousine

Hitching east of Vegas, I pointed my thumb
north to the clouds when a paisley Mercedes Benz
limo screeched to stop on a scorched stretch
of highway. Its rear door opened to my skinny self.
A voice yelled, *Sugar, wiggle those thumbs in here*
before I come out and plop you onto my hot lap.

I hurried to the car, sat between Lucille with the hot lap
and Conan, all six feet four of him and his huge thumbs.
No barbarian, he whispered in a tone I could barely hear
to Ginger, Jessica, Nicole, *Give this boy a benze-*
drine before he falls over, under and out from himself.
Hey, don't laugh, Conan told them, *it's no stretch!*

Jessica stole the action from Conan, began to stretch,
cascades of hair flowing down shoulders into her lap,
Don't worry, babe, it's not like we'll hurt your little ole self
or any of you. It's just that Ginger saw your thumb
in the desert and felt you'd like whooping it up in the Benz,
plus Nicole wants to cuddle with you, and hear

you breathe, hear you smile and dream. So you're here!
I couldn't believe this crew beyond the wildest stretch
of my fantasies: five redheaded, sequined drunks in a Benz—
with huge hands and hundred-dollar bills, snorting coke on laps—
who fascinated me, a hitcher in the desert with sexy thumbs!
And I loved the way they enjoyed themselves

with a stranger who didn't know them, much less himself.
I asked them about their gigs and why they were here.
All five laughed, sang as one, *Because of your thumbs!*
Then Nicole cooed, *Baby, why not stretch*
a little, close your eyes. I'll give you a doozy of a lap
dance everyone dreams about getting in wacky Benzes.

Woozy, drifting under the sea—with the possible bends—
I resisted sleep to party with the five redheads, despite myself.
I craved the time of my life, one that fell into my lap,
one that told me I'd regret not enjoying luck as it came, here
and now, Nicole urging, *Kiss me, hon!* I felt a hard stretch.
No, not *that*—but Ginger, Lucille sucking my thumbs!

In the Benz they advised me, a redhead, why I was here:
to find myself with celebrity impersonators in stretch
limos, to enjoy lap dances and sucking on thumbs.

Strangers Keep Friending Me

on Facebook. Sometimes they're women
wanting boyfriends. Because I'm a cynic,
I delete some requests, mark them as spam.
They wouldn't date an old man with a cat,
even if it's a calico. And people who share
mutual friends with me—friends I barely know—

friend me. I don't have the heart to click *No,*
write, *I can't be your friend, even if you're a woman*
with blonde hair, green eyes and stories to share,
not to mention big dreams that'd cure a cynic
like me. And what if you discover I own ten cats
whose favorite foods are pepperoni and Spam?

Plus, my favorite Broadway show is "Spam-
alot"? I've thought about Facebook and know
scam artists target me, my calico cat,
even my wife, for she's a generous woman:
somebody posed as a Marine—a cynic,
I'm sure—and friended her, claimed he wanted to share

his life with her, maybe because she called herself Sherri,
writing, *Hi, I'm Sherri from Cincinnati and love Spam.*
The soldier—I'd guess a Nigerian and a clumsy cynic—
unfriended Sherri without a word, didn't know
she lied a little when she wrote, *Whoa, man,*
I'm just an old lover of long-haired calico cats.

Many amazing, awesome, cool cats
use Facebook—I'm friends with 4,000 I share
nothing with, though some are women
who swig Cutty Sark with their Spam—
and all of them can say words like *No*
because they choose the path of cynics

who've survived by acting cynical.
They want friendship like cats
that approach people who can't say *No*,
that choose animal lovers willing to share
their food, whether pepperoni or Spam.
Strangers who think men tougher marks than women.

Call me a cynic, though you know I share
pictures of my cat drinking milk with her Spam.
But do you know whether I'm a man or a woman?

The Arch Manipulator

A teacher bragged to me in his sports
car that he dubbed himself the Arch
Manipulator. Before I asked him to elaborate
he recited an erudite poem by Auden
I can't recall any more than the moon
with her cratered face remembers her man.

I knew this poser would never man
up to his self-indulgent title, any more than I'd sport
a face with craters like those on the moon,
who once a month smiles a smile so arch
I search for that enigmatic poem by Auden
and laugh at myself for failing to see elaborate

lie-truths the teacher told his students: *Never elaborate*
in a poem what it feels like to be a woman or a man,
and don't imitate poets who imitate life, like Auden—
just write banal poems that need writing, such as sports
poems, he said with his trademarked arch
of a sneer. Like the distant, beautiful moon's,

the adored moon, the mythologized moon, the moon
we shoot at each other when failing to elaborate
vulgar messages. We convey them by the arches
of McDonald's, built by a businessman
named Kroc, who wore a tie, white shirt and sport
coat. He reminded me of Auden,

who, if he ate a double cheese, wouldn't be Auden,
would he, though it resembles the cratered moon?
Maybe Auden, like the teacher and Kroc, drove a sports
car—an MG with decals of the Muse so elaborate
it'd be the envy of every moonless man
who'd never dream of naming himself the Arch

Manipulator. Unless he saw himself arch
in an ironic way, much like Auden
would if he compared himself to the man
abandoned by the crater-faced moon,
who smiles at us after we ask her to elaborate
on her silent riddle, forgetting men: *My sole sport.*

With an arch smile each month, the crater-faced moon
(she's the Arch Manipulator, not Auden) won't elaborate
when intimating she ignores the man in her for sport.

The Bargain

Two photographers staggered into a Bowery dive
dubbed by its owner *The Dark Side*.
One a slim woman, followed by a wide man—
his name Weegee, hers Diane—
into a hellhole disguised as a ship's room
smelling of Schlitz, Old Crow and tuna fish.

Above the mirror a mounted swordfish,
one that had failed to dive
to the depths of its ocean room.
Pouring drinks, the bartender sighed
every time the offbeat snapper Diane
stumbled into his bar with a man.

Tonight, not just any man,
but a genius who loved to fish
for dead bodies, while Lady Diane
never resisted or declined an endive
when proffered by a dwarf at her side
rubbing his eyes free of rheum.

This evening, in the overheated room,
an idea formed in the bulb of Weegee Man:
he asked his date to play dead on her side,
pretend to be a three-day-old fish
that forgot to ignore the hook and nosedived
to the sea bottom, near a wreck, *The Diane*.

The proposal appealed to Diane,
who wanted to see Weegee in a dark room
and sacrifice his control to take a dive
for her sake, and Weegee Man
viewed Lady Diane as a unique fish,
one that could inspire his artistic side.

Deal, she replied, *but after we do that outside,*
I'll be Weegee and you Diane
in matching smocks that reek of tuna fish
smellier than this lame room.
Ambitious Weegee considered himself a man
but agreed to take a feminine dive.

Two photographers shambled outside from the room:
Dark Diane agreed to the wish of Weegee Man,
who later portrayed a twin girl able to fish and dive.

for Roberta Greifer

Wanda and Henry

My neighbors are lawyers,
the wife known as Wanda
Wallace. Her husband's name? Henry
Hallahan. They claim they're Danes,
and possess enough drive
to make saltine crackers

blush. I think they're crackers:
because they're high-powered lawyers
doesn't mean they dislike screwing at drive-
in movies. The next day 300-lb Wanda
told me she identified with the Danish
actress because she didn't like to hurry

when it came to coming together with Henry.
To further the delay, she loved eating crackers
on her back. And the post-coital dessert? Danish
pastries so sweet they made her a liar.
And her voice a magic wand, a
rhythm to it that made her husband drive

into her again, until he wanted title of driver
in their sex crashes. How about horny Henry?
Let's focus on aptly named Moby Wanda.
After winning a trial, she ate graham crackers
to celebrate with friends—lawyers
taking turns riding Radiohead, her Great Dane,

except Wanda, who knew she couldn't ride the Dane.
Instead, she sneaked into her Ferrari, driving
to the Blue Ridge Mountains, where her lawyer
father lived, to complain about shrimp-sized Henry
and his refusal to join her for snacks of Cracker
Jacks, four papayas, jerky, a loaf of Wonder

Bread and a jar of Skippy. Her father said, *Wanda,*
stop acting American and be a Dane.
Don't eat like a Georgia Cracker
out of shape, show me that law-school drive
of yours before you met sorry-assed Henry,
who's the South's lousiest lawyer.

A year later, 100-lb Wanda regained her drive.
She met Hemming, another Dane, divorced Henry,
who built a cracker factory and married a tax lawyer.

Bill, Herman, Chip and the Twins

Bill, a guy I know, calls himself Chip.
He's from Kansas, flashes a widow's peak
the envy of friends, all weasels.
Chip eats peanut brittle and pears
before he steps into the ring to box,
loving to punch his opponent's shoulders.

His friends joke about Bill's shoulder,
saying, *Man, you gotta get rid of that chip*
or a sparring partner might box
you into a corner. Then you'll feel piqued
and act like a spoiled au pair—
or worse, you'll sing Pop Goes the Weasel.

Laughing at him—their little weasel,
they call him—they see he can't shoulder
much derision, unlike his peers
in Congress. Colleagues chip
at his ego, because they peek
into his frail psyche, but Bill doesn't box

himself in, challenging all 434 to box
him. They refuse: these weasels
shirk courage in times of Bill's pique.
Instead, they offer barbecued shoulder
and his favorite chocolate chip
cookies. Sometimes he opts for pears

so he's virile when he beds a pair
of sisters. Inviting them into his box
of a house, he says, *Call me Chip,*
and they fondle Herman, his pet weasel.
They rub the little guy's tummy and shoulder,
and, as their foreplay reaches its peak,

Bill frowns at all three in a fit of pique.
As a Romeo, Herman has no peer:
this is too much for Bill to shoulder,
so he challenges Herman and the twins to box,
but Herman, an evolved weasel,
elopes with his new girlfriends, away from Chip,

to Pikes Peak, where they grow evergreen box
shrubs and parent a pair of wrestling weasels
named Barbecued Soldier and Computer Chip.

Harry the Hippie

Sometimes I wish I lived in Michigan.
I think of it as the land of lakes and smoke,
of Honey Crisp apples and exotic incense.
My one visit there is less than vivid:
In fact, it was of no consequence,
because it happened before bombs,

before I met Harry, a hippie, a walking bomb.
He drove to New Jersey from Michigan—
after that he lived in Truth or Consequences,
where the law busted him for smoking
peyote. He told me later of vivid
visions he enhanced with incense.

In Jersey, he grew angry and incensed
at the Vietnam War, joined a few bombers
who called themselves *Warriors for the Livid*
and hijacked a Trailways to Michigan.
Its engine died of thirst, too much smoke,
in Detroit, and the hippies consequentially

scattered everywhere. One consequence
followed another. Harry, incensed
at his arrest because of smoke,
escaped to construct crude bombs,
exploding one in Ypsilanti, Michigan.
My memory isn't that vivid

but Harry told me something vivid:
I don't give a fuck about consequences,
but I'm getting the hell out of Michigan.
Harry left for Cuba, the cops trailed the incense
that followed him, but he and his infamous bombs
disappeared in a whirlwind of fire and smoke.

When Harry returned, when he thought the smoke
had scattered and his life changed, it became vivid
once again: sentenced to prison for making bombs,
he served time, learned about consequences
and life's value in dollars and in cents.
After the iron gates opened, he thumbed to Michigan,

bought a head shop called *Smoky Consequences*
with his wife, Vivian, who knew he adored incense,
and forgot about bombs because they loved Michigan.

History of a Bigot

I never learned to love
a butterfly's wings, the ripple of wavy hair.
My old man numbed me with buckles of belts,
along with barbed-wire insults and blame
he loved to wrap around my sensitive head.
He watched with glee when I winced and cried,

a weak kid. As an adolescent I didn't cry
but with those lack of tears I couldn't love
myself anymore than a turtle that swallows its head.
I began my journey of odium by growing long hair:
I felt kinship with hippies who blamed
society for their alienated rage and dodged belts

from fathers who thought nothing of belts
of Jimmy Beam and Johnny Black before they cried
and always found their sons to blame
for being losers in life and love.
Ten years later, I buzz cut my hair,
joined a gang of skinheads

who grunged guitars and cracked heads.
This didn't happen in Frisco, but the Cotton Belt,
where haters despised long hair and short hair,
but I loathed rednecks— they never cried,
didn't know the meaning of love
since they never accepted self-blame.

As children, their mothers told them, *I blame
you, I ought to bash your stupid head
in.* Fifteen years later, I still didn't know love,
so I joined right-wing crackpots who swung belts
at smaller victims, young men we kicked until they cried,
slashing their faces with swastikas, hacking their hair.

Twenty years later, I wonder what happened to my hair.
If I could, I'd find some cretin to cut with blame.
I'd feel better if the whiner whimpered and cried.
Then I'd notch it up and grind his head,
tie up his arms with rusty chains, poison-laced belts,
and after I finished him, I'd call his death my act of love.

I'm not prejudiced. I hate everybody: long hair, bald head.
Who cares, as long as I can blame and whip with a belt?
I can't cry. I hate myself. I think I'll buy a gun to love.

Ballad in Plain F of Orange Head,
Cher and Stackalee

Jack Frost leaned into the *Idiot Wind* bar
after I told him I'd be sitting in a yellow chair,
chatting up Mona, Isis, Donnie the orange head.
Hurricane, the waiter, jotted down our drinks:
Mona a Highway Blues, Isis a Frozen Mary.
Jack and I craved a Thin Man, Donnie a mirror.

Stackalee swaggered in with gypsy gal Lili and a meer-
cat, Baby Blue, in a Panama hat, nibbling a Mounds bar.
Drinking, recounting stories about Baby Blue, merry,
the duo bought pickled eggs from bald barmaid Cher,
who joked, *What's Baby Blue gonna drink?*
Stackalee muttered, *A root beer with a lotta head.*

We snickered, except Donnie the orange head,
loudmouth and raccoon hands groping for a mirror.
Jack Frost offered Donnie a kickass drink.
Thanks, man! I'll whirl over to the bar.
Pushing his heels, half-lounging in his swivel chair,
he ordered Cher, *Baldy, gimme a drink I'll marry.*

Cher didn't like that, said, *Alrighty, Orange Mary,*
and, flames in her eyes, poured Pabst over his head
as the room applauded, jeered the buffoon in the chair,
who left for the john, combed his hair in the mirror.
I'm great, he told himself, pushed back to the bar,
slowly asking Cher to make an ass-kicking drink.

Cher mixed Donnie a belladonna-bourbon drink,
warning him in a stern tone, *You can marry
this, but call me Baldy, I'll conk ya with my crowbar.*
He smiled, *Believe me, I wanna keep my head.
I know you run this fabulous place—I'm a mere
mortal—so I'll mosey to the table in my chair.*

Cher glared at Orange Head in the swivel chair,
who, returning to the table with a red face and drink,
growled at Baby Blue, *You're too ugly for a mirror,*
and knocked off her Panama hat: *Can I call you Mary?*
Lili screamed, *I'm gonna smack your fuckin' head!*
Yo, Cher, toss me that goddamned crowbar!

Stackalee didn't need a crowbar. Sitting in his chair,
he pointed a Glock at the buffoon's head, gulped a drink,
and trumped Donnie, who loved to marry a mirror.

Pumpkin Man

His name alone is an October
cartoon, but he's an omen
that warns us like a hawk
swooping above black snakes
unluckier than the thirteenth
disciple who hovers like a specter.

Infamous Pumpkin Man isn't a specter,
but he's full of the famed October
surprises that fall on Friday the 13th,
standing in cornfields, yelling, *Oh men,*
oh women, kill the snakes,
hang women who hawk

their wares at night and hock
their babies' souls. No, he isn't a specter,
but chilling as a coral snake
that strikes on the last day of October.
Pumpkin Man's more than an omen:
he's the personification of the number 13,

betrays friends with his straw heart, as the thirteenth
disciple did at the last supper. He's the hawk's
nemesis, the hawk unafraid of human omens,
fearless of pumpkin men fearful of specters,
especially on the last day of golden October,
the day of lizards, of alligators, of orange snakes.

One day, it's foretold, a ghostly savior will snake
with a plumber's auger the second to the thirteenth
straw in Pumpkin Man's brain, October-
colored, like his hair that barkers have hawked
as a brand. It's immortal as a specter's
mastery of spells, sacrifices and omens

that belie the trust of women and men.
And Pumpkin Man, alone in the field, will sneak,
or try to sneak, away in his final days like a specter
from a graveyard, and the twelfth and thirteenth
members of a boil of spiraling hawks will
grab his long red tie on the last day of golden October,

strangling him as no omen can, the thirteenth
and last time specters roam the days of October
that celebrate with the world, the snakes, the hawks.

Sestinas Bad and Good

Another sestina about sestinas—good and bad.
Most people don't read them, some poets don't write
them. Beats me: great fun, kaleidoscope glass
to study while I search for and play with six precise words.
They please me before I tell myself I'm not a snob
when I write them. I admire sestiners Denise Duhamel,

Bishop, Ashbery, Cummins, Lehman and Denise Duhamel
(I mention Duhamel twice since she writes extra good
double sestinas, poems I won't tackle—I'd look like a slob
on paper). Let's face it, mayhem ensues when writing
sestinas, for the order of specific words
in correct places is difficult as crafting stained glass

windows, plus clarity is an important element of glass,
such as the crystal clear "Sestina" by Elizabeth Bishop,
who didn't play, but worked, at choosing words
that matter when judging a sestina good or bad.
She knew finding them for sestinas was a rite
every poet drives through—whether in a Peugeot or a Saab.

That, odd as it sounds, is like asking children not to sob
when forcing them to stand in straight lines by beveled glass,
then deciding whether they're in the wrong or right
spot. Another poet who's one of the best at this is John Ashbery,
who I never thought would compose a sestina so good
about Popeye with a surreal combination of cartoonish words

that I'd grin, shake my head and be at such a word
loss I'd jump in my Peugeot and eat two Subs.
Bad sandwiches rather than good.
Who knows, maybe they won't taste like crushed glass
in my mouth while I read *The Whole Truth* by James Cummins,
a book of sestinas about Perry Mason and pals he wrote

decades ago, when I read it the first time. What a writer!
His Perry was funny, sharp, a lawyer who assembled words
for a jury in such a way that'd impress even David Lehman,
who tackles the big, unwieldy boat that the sestina is and swabs
its deck, polishes its wood, sets its sail, twirls its wheel, cleans glass
of the portholes so the pleased reader thinks it's better than bad.

I trust I haven't written this sestina like a slob or a snob.
I hope—maybe incorrectly—my words are clear as glass.
If not, I'll ask Denise whether she thinks it's good or bad.

Sestina Stalker

On the computer, chomping a celery stalk
with tomato juice six days ago,
I stumbled onto a site devoted to sestinas,
found a chat room, discussed pros and cons
of the form with a faceless body of black letters
who wanted nothing but to write and praise

that medieval verse from Provence. I prayed
this person wasn't a predator who'd stalk
someone who answered her rambling letters
by changing subjects to hip-hop or go-go
dancing's allure among cons.
Trouble brewed when she called herself *Sestina*:

She said, *I think you should go by* Sestina,
too. Believe me, Bobo, if you don't, pray
my buddy doesn't hurt you, a big ex-con
everybody's afraid of called Boston Beanstalk
who'll tell you to give suicide a go
once he barrages you with calls and letters.

If I want, he'll brand you with letters—
yes, you guessed it, Bobo, S E S T I N A—
on your forehead so deep you'll have to go
visit a plastic surgeon or a priest you can pray
to in confession. Or your cane can be a stalk.
I tried to bluff, bragged my brother could con

the frown off anybody she knew, even ex-cons.
She laughed so hard onscreen that letters
bounced harder than inept stalkers
fleeing this woman named *Sestina*
who hunts for sad sack poets she can prey
upon, sad sack poets too dense to play Go.

I'm still in the dire world I was days ago:
this psycho who brags of poets she's conned
into loving a poem she claims is worthy of praise
threatens to e-mail on random days, expects letters
every week and a poem to her every night, a sestina,
and only then will she *think* about others to stalk.

I'll give it a go: with black wit I'll write letters.
I'll con my brother into writing sestinas for Sestina
and hope she finds other victims to love and stalk.

Mad Sestina King

I'm the Mad Sestina King.
Sestinas haunt me every day.
People laugh, claim I'm a fool.
Sestinas cackle like magpies
about my obsessions.
Such as: Mad Sestina Queen, do you exist?

Do you feel your sole reason to exist
is to write sestinas about me, Mad King,
or another fascinating obsession?
Will you survive a sunless day
when sestinas don't chatter like magpies?
I sometimes think I'm a mad sestina fool,

but to write haiku would prove more foolish
because they're so short they barely exist,
like momentary silence from the magpie.
I'll claim I'm the Mad Sestina King
until I'm depleted of words like *day*.
That'll never happen—I'm too obsessive

and love to write in a spiral of obsessions
as long as I don't appear fool-
hardy. As long as I'm challenged by day-
in day-out sestina-writing existence,
as long as I'm the Mad Sestina King,
until sestinas cackle at me like magpies

Heckle and Jeckle, who call me a magpie
in my dreams, tell me I'm too obsessive,
that I'm not the Mad Sestina King.
They call me the worst kind of fool,
a sestina writer in an existential
crisis, one who'll never win the day

until he writes a sestina every day
to prove he's worthwhile. Magpies,
calm down! You sestinas are real, exist
in your glory, like most objects of obsession.
So, you out there, call me a fool,
unless you're Queen to my Mad Sestina King.

Every day, I chase obsessions.
I listen to magpies. They're not fools.
They exist for me, the Mad Sestina King.

Notes

"Elegy for a Rock 'n' Roll Life" incorporates phrases from Lou Reed's songs.

"Ballad in Plain F of Orange Head, Cher and Stackalee" appropriates characters from Bob Dylan's songs.

Acknowledgments

The author wishes to thank the editors of the journals in which the poems below have been published, sometimes in earlier versions and with different titles:

Chiron Review: "Elegy for a Rock 'n' Roll Life," "If You Might Be Dying"
CircleShow: "The Bargain," "The Mermaid and the Airplane"
Easy Street: "Mad Sestina King"
The Ginger Collect: "Ginger Woman," "He Called Himself *Smart*"
The HitchLit Review: "The Master and Her Artists"
In Between Hangovers: "Femme Fatale," "Redhead Limousine"
The Magnolia Review: "In My Younger Years I Loved the Oboe"
Midnight Lane Boutique: "Ballad in Plain F of Orange Head, Cher and Stackalee"
The New Verse News: "Pumpkin Man"
Third Wednesday: "The Arch Manipulator"
Yellow Mama: "Harry the Hippie," "Michelangelo's Handshakes," "Strangers Keep Friending Me," "Word Cruncher"
Your One Phone Call: "Sestina Stalker"

I'd like to thank Kim Addonizio for dubbing me "The Mad Sestina King," using that image from Adam LeFevre's poem "Sestina Sestina."

I owe a very special thank you to the late Joan Colby, with whom I exchanged end words for a number of the poems in this collection and from whom I learned a great deal about the craft of composing sestinas.

About FutureCycle Press

FutureCycle Press is dedicated to publishing lasting English-language poetry in both print-on-demand and Kindle formats. Founded in 2007 by long-time independent editor/publishers and partners Diane Kistner and Robert S. King, the press incorporated as a nonprofit in 2012. A number of our editors are distinguished poets and writers in their own right, and we have been actively involved in the small press movement going back to the early seventies.

We award the FutureCycle Poetry Book Prize and honorarium annually for the best full-length volume of poetry we published that year. Introduced in 2013, proceeds from our Good Works projects are donated to charity. Our Selected Poems series highlights contemporary poets with a substantial body of work to their credit; with this series we strive to resurrect work that has had limited distribution and is now out of print.

We are dedicated to giving all of the authors we publish the care their work deserves, offering a catalog of the most diverse and distinguished work possible, and paying forward any earnings to fund more great books. All of our books are kept "alive" and available unless and until an author requests a title be taken out of print.

We've learned a few things about independent publishing over the years. We've also evolved a unique, resilient publishing model that allows us to focus mainly on vetting and preserving for posterity poetry collections of exceptional quality without becoming overwhelmed with bookkeeping and mailing, fundraising activities, or taxing editorial and production "bubbles." To find out more about what we are doing, come see us at www.futurecycle.org.

The FutureCycle Poetry Book Prize

All full-length volumes of poetry published by FutureCycle Press in a calendar year are considered for the annual FutureCycle Poetry Book Prize. This allows us to consider each submission on its own merits, outside of the context of a traditional contest. Too, the judges see the finished book, which will have benefitted from the beautiful book design and strong editorial gloss we're famous for.

The book ranked the best in judging is announced as the prize-winner in the subsequent year. There is no fixed monetary award; instead, the winning poet receives an honorarium of 20% of the total net royalties from all poetry books and chapbooks the press sold online in the year the winning book was published. The winner is also accorded the honor of being on the panel of judges for the next year's competition; all judges receive copies of all contending books to keep for their personal library.